Wild Edible Plants of Idaho

Lincoln Town Press
All rights reserved

Copyright © 2023, 2025 by Charles W. Kane
First edition, Second printing

Library of Congress Control Number: 2022952281
ISBN 10: 173692415X and ISBN 13: 9781736924150

No part of this book may be reproduced or transmitted in any form or by any means, electronic or mechanical, including photocopying, recording, or by any information storage and retrieval system, without written permission from the publisher.

Wild Edible Plants of Idaho is intended solely for educational purposes. The publisher and author disclaim any liability arising from the use of any plant listed in this book.

Printed on 100% recycled paper

Introduction	2	Huckleberry	23	Sheep's Sorrel	43
Amaranth	4	Indian Rice Grass	24	Sow Thistle	44
Asparagus	5	Lambsquarters	25	Springparsley	45
Beeplant	6	Mallow	26	Thimbleberry	46
Biscuitroot	7	Maple	27	Thistle	47
Bitterroot	8	Mariposa Lily	28	Tuber Starwort	48
Blackberry	9	Miner's Lettuce	29	Tule	49
Bracken Fern	10	Monkey Flower	30	Tumble Mustard	50
Camas	11	Mulberry	31	Utah Honeysuckle	51
Checkermallow	12	Mullein	32	Watercress	52
Chickweed	13	Nettle	33	Western Spring Beauty	53
Chokecherry	14	Orach	34	Wild Onion	54
Currant	15	Ox-Eye Daisy	35	Wild Rose	55
Elder	16	Panicgrass	36	Wild Strawberry	56
Fairybells	17	Pellitory	37	Wild Sunflower	57
Field Pennycress	18	Plantain	38	Wintercress	58
Glacier Lily	19	Raspberry	39	Yellow Fritillary	59
Gooseberry	20	Russian Olive	40	Yellowdock	60
Hawthorn	21	Salsify	41	Yampah	61
Hollygrape	22	Serviceberry	42	Index	62

Introduction

Idaho's Wild Edible Flora

Idaho enjoys the interplay of several main topographic and climatic influences: Rocky Mountains to the east, river basins to the west, Pacific atmospheric currents to the north and west, and continental weather to the south. This mixture of elements creates a dynamic and non-monolithic underpinning. Consequentiality, the state's plant life is varied.

The plants of the higher mountains (Bitterroots, Salmon River Mountains, and so forth) are known for their intense flurry of activity over a span of several months, mainly due to a short growing season. Accordingly, during the summertime at high elevations, there is no want of Rose family fruits and leafy greens. What the mountains lack in species diversity, they make up for in quantity. The river bottoms and surrounding plains, hills and transition zones host more significant numbers of utilitarian plants. Native grass seed, Ribes fruit, and a bevy of edible bulbs and greens are found here. All zones are important; however, like other western mountain states, below alpine/subalpine elevations holds the most value for the forager.

What is a Wild Edible Plant?

A wild edible should be considered more than simply a plant (or plant part) that can be chewed and swallow without harm or benefit (in other words, a 'neutral' plant). Nor is it one that is medicinal (high in physiologically-influencing compounds). It certainly is not a poisonous plant (very high in these compounds). A true wild edible plant is one that contains calories (and nutrients), but very few to no physiologically-influencing compounds, or through mild processing can made safe.

Poisonous **Medicinal** **Neutral** **Wild-Edible** **Garden/Crop**

Environmental Concerns & Legalities

None of the plants listed are threatened or endangered. In fact, many of them are considered weeds. If a species is encountered in a less-than-ideal situation, this mainly due to environmental stress or edge-of-range habitat, it may be worth considering letting the group go undisturbed.

Is plant collection on 'public' land legal? It's complicated. Technically, it's mostly illegal. But is it wrong? These two things are not the same. Without getting into a more involved ideological discussion, if engaged in respectfully and sensibly, it's like driving 1 mph over the speed limit...there's no harm done of consequence. The botanical repercussions of grazing, logging, and mining (legal on many tax-payer funded but government administered lands), or even what a heavy rain washes away, in any given period of time, far, far, far surpasses foraging activity. Take heed though, describing this point to a power-tripping ticket-happy forest ranger or virtue-signaling suburban eco-Karen may be a hard sell.

Proper Identification

It's a wise idea to know without a doubt what is being consumed prior to its consumption. Besides this publication, I recommend the use of a field guide (or two) to confirm species identification. Most of the time, cases of mistaken identity will not cause serious harm. However, mistakes with Carrot, Lily, and Nightshade family plants may be deadly.

Resources & Acknowledgments

For supportive classification/distribution information, I referred to the SEINet database, Flora of North America (via efloras.org), and Biota of North America Program site. CC/Public Domain photos: 'Lewisia pygmaea' by John Game, CC BY-SA 2.0. 'Lewisia rediviva' by Stan Shebs, CC BY-SA 3.0. 'Camassia quamash 1 and 2' by Walter Siegmund, CC-SA 2.0. 'Erythronium grandiflorum' by Jason Hollinger, CC BY 2.0. 'Erythronium grandiflorum' by Thayne Tuason, CC BY-SA 4.0. 'Vaccinium membranaceum 1 and 2' by Katja Schulz, CC BY 2.0. 'Parietaria pensylvanica 1 and 2' by F.D. Richards, CC BY-SA 2.0. 'Cymopterus terebinthinus' by Brewbooks, CC BY-SA 2.0. 'Longstalk springparsley' by Andrey Zharkikh, CC BY-SA 2.0. 'Claytonia lanceolata' by Thayne Tuason, CC BY-SA 4.0. 'Claytonia lanceolata' by Jacopo Werther, CC BY-SA 2.0. 'Fritillaria pudica' by Matt Lavin, CC BY-SA 2.0. 'Fritillaria pudica' by Thayne Tuason, CC BY-SA 4.0.

Poisonous Plants

The following are a small number of problematic genera found in Idaho. This is by no means a complete list.

Monkshood (Aconitum)	Deathcamas (Anticlea)	Dogbane (Apocynum)
Water hemlock (Cicuta)	Water hemlock (Cicuta)	Poison hemlock (Conium)
Poison hemlock (Conium)	Henbane (Hyoscyamus)	False hellebore (Veratrum)

SUMMER — **HERBACEOUS PARTS/SEED**

Amaranth
Amaranthus spp.

Other Common Names
Tumbleweed amaranth, Prostrate pigweed, Powell's amaranth, etc.

Range & Habitat
Idaho is home to about six species of Amaranthus, though only several are abundant. All are common to disturbed soils such as old fields, ditches, and roadsides. They need full sun and somewhat moist soils to thrive.

Edible Uses
The young leaves of the larger/upright species can be eaten raw (as a forage/salad) early in the season. However, all members are best utilized as a cooked green. A quick boil and freshwater rinse will eliminate some of the plant's oxalate content and make the leaves more palatable so larger quantities can be consumed. Once cooked, the leaves taste much like spinach.

After Amaranth has gone to seed (late summer–fall), strip the dried seed spikes from the top of each plant. Wearing gloves, rub the clusters together to separate the seeds from their spiky encasements. Winnow the seeds from the chaff in a light breeze or fan set on low. The seeds are high in protein and generally nutritious. They can be ground into a meal, cooked like other grains, or soaked and then eaten.

Medicinal Uses
There are no significant medicinal uses for Amaranth.

Cautions & Special Note
Be sure to boil and rinse the leaves if consuming them in larger amounts. This removes some of their oxalate content. Cultivated species were once important Mesoamerican food (seed) crops.

Sustenance Index: High
Pictured: *Amaranthus hybridus (top) | Amaranthus palmeri (bottom)*

SPRING | **SPEAR**

Asparagus
Asparagus officinalis

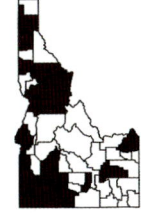

Other Common Names
Common asparagus, Garden asparagus, Wild asparagus

Range & Habitat
Asparagus officinalis is a non-native garden/crop cultivar that has escaped its original boundaries and is now found in disturbed and lower-lying/moist soils. A people-plant, it tends not to grows in the wilds, but rather around population centers. Look to field margins, grassy areas, road and trail sides, and untended embankments.

Edible Uses
Clip the emerging spears in the spring. They should be flexible and non-woody. If allowed to grow un-cut the spears develop into the plant's stems and are non-edible.

Steam/sauté/boil 'wild' Asparagus spears like the garden-grown/store-bought kind. Seasoned with a little butter and spices they will be equally delicious and nutritious.

Medicinal Uses
The root tea is a traditional European herbal remedy for gout, uric acid-type kidney stones, related joint inflammation, and generally overly-acidic urine (imagine a historical cold season western European diet of beef, wheat, and wine/ale).

Cautions & Special Note
Aside from sulfur-smelling urine, there are no cautions for Asparagus consumption.

The spears contain asparagusic acid, which some people after digesting, metabolize into methanethiol, dimethyl sulfide, and other sulfur-based compounds. These are responsible for the Asparagus-smelling urine noticeable after the plant's consumption. Purple cultivars of Asparagus are much higher in antioxidant pigments (anthocyanins) than standard types.

Sustenance Index: Medium
Pictured: *Asparagus officinalis*

SUMMER — LEAF/POD/SEED

Beeplant
Peritoma serrulata (Cleome serrulata)

Other Common Names
Rocky Mountain beeplant, Bee spiderflower

Range & Habitat
Beeplant is a large annual herb of the western mountain states. It's found below the high mountains in disturbed soils: next to dirt roadsides, trailsides, and drainage bottoms/sides. It's a fast grower in response to summertime rains.

Edible Uses
The young leaves, flowers, and pods (green/flexible) are gathered mid-summer. Eat these parts fresh (limited) as a spicy/mustard-like salad addition. Better yet, simmer them for 5–10 minutes and rinse with fresh water. Season to taste and eat solo as a cooked green or add Beeplant to other cooked greens as part of a combo.

The young pods (seeds still unformed) are pickled like capers, though this will remove much of the pod's natural spiciness. The mature seeds too are edible. They're best soaked, rinsed, dehydrated, ground, and then added in small amounts to other flours.

Medicinal Uses & Cautions
Beeplant is not significantly medicinal, nor are there any cautions for the plant (aside from cautions common to all mustard oil containing plants – see Wintercress).

Special Note
Most American Indians (if regionally common) utilized Beeplant as an edible due to its abundance and non-toxicity. Like Mustard, Beeplant's spiciness is due to its glucosinolate content.

Sustenance Index: Medium
Pictured: *Peritoma serrulata*

SPRING–SUMMER — **WHOLE PLANT**

Biscuitroot
Lomatium bicolor, L. cous, L. foeniculaceum, L nudicaule. L. triternatum, etc.

Other Common Names
Wasatch desertparsley, Cous biscuitroot, Carrotleaf desertparsley, Barestem biscuitroot, Nineleaf springparsley, and so forth

Range & Habitat
All Lomatium species are alternatively named Biscuitroot, Desertparsley, and/or Springparsley. About 2–dozen species are found in Idaho. They are common to most of the state's vegetation/elevation zones and prefer rocky hillsides and slopes.

Edible Uses
Most species of Biscuitroot are edible, not medicinal (see below). The leaf, stem, seed, and root are all palatable. The herbaceous portions are best chopped and boiled/sautéed as a cooked green prior to consumption. They're not bad tasting consumed fresh, but they may be a little fibrous/aromatic/mildly bitter. The thickened and non–woody small roots are starchy and bland-tasting, similar to a parsnip. When fresh they can be a mildly bitter; however, boiling/rinsing renders them more palatable. They are a good complex carbohydrate source.

Medicinal Uses, Cautions, & Special Note
Medicinal species of Biscuitroot (of which there are a handful) tend to be bigger plants, with bitter/resinous roots. When the fresh roots of these species are injured, they tend to weep a sticky latex. The roots of edible species are non–resinous and comparatively smaller. Lomatium dissectum represents the most common medicinal species of the genus. The root is an important lung medicine, particularly if a viral element is present. There are no cautions for Biscuitroot's edible use. Lomatium is related to Fennel (edible and medicinal), Poison hemlock, and Water hemlock. The last two plants are potentially deadly. Be certain of positive identification prior to this plant's utilization.

Sustenance Index: Medium
Pictured: *Lomatium nevadense*

SPRING–SUMMER   **ENTIRE PLANT**

Bitterroot
Lewisia nevadensis, L. pygmaea, L. rediviva, L. triphylla

Other Common Names
Nevada bitterroot, Sierra bitterroot, Pygmy bitterroot, Alpine bitterroot, Oregon bitterroot, Three-leaved lewisia

Range & Habitat
Bitterroot is a western-growing small perennial. Nearly two-dozen species comprise the genus, however in Idaho only four species are common enough to warrant edible recognition. Lewisia nevadensis (Nevada BR), L. pygmaea (Pygmy BR), and L. triphylla (3-leaved BR) are alpine/mountain/high-meadow plants. Lewisia rediviva is found lower in elevation, but not that low (it's absent from the plains/river-bottoms).

Edible Uses
Bitterroot is a well-known traditional Native American forage plant. Most tribes utilized it to some degree if it was in their proximity. The above-ground parts are semi-succulent and tender. They need little processing, so their addition to salads or as a simple forage is well founded. The roots are tender but semi-fibrous (not woody) forked taproots. Although usually bland in taste, older plants often produce roots that are a little acrid. Whatever the taste, they are best chopped and simmered for 5–10 minutes, rinsed, and seasoned prior to consumption.

Medicinal Uses, Cautions, & Special Note
There are no medicinal uses for Bitterroot. The plant does have some oxalate content; however, if consumed in non-insane amounts, there is little reason to be concerned. Bitterroot belongs to the Miner's lettuce family (Montiaceae). Other members include Miner's lettuce and Western spring beauty. Accordingly, edible uses are similar. Idaho's Bitterroot Mountains are in fact named after the plant. More than four species call the range their home.

Sustenance Index: Medium
Pictured: *Lewisia pygmaea (top) | Lewisia rediviva (bottom)*

SUMMER | FRUIT

Blackberry
Rubus armeniacus, R. laciniatus, R. ursinus

Other Common Names
Himalayan blackberry, Cut-leaf blackberry, Pacific blackberry

Range & Habitat
Several Blackberry species are present in central-northern Idaho. Himalayan blackberry (Rubus armeniacus) has the most widespread potential. Although not native to North America, it does well in an array of habitats since escaping cultivation. All species prefer rich/moist soils and sun, so look for the plant in canyon bottoms, around streamsides, and along forest/field edges.

Edible Uses
When ripe, Blackberry fruit (not an actual berry but a drupe) are dark purple to black, and usually smaller than store-bought. They are sweet, mildly tart, and delicious when gathered from a healthy and well-hydrated specimen.

Eat the fruit raw directly from the plant or prepare them in the form of a jelly or fruit spread. They can too be dehydrated and reconstituted for later use. Blackberry is a good source of vitamins C and A, magnesium, and health-promoting pigments.

Medicinal Uses, Cautions, & Special Note
Blackberry leaf is a medicinal equivalent to Raspberry leaf, which means the leaf tea is internally used as a mild female reproductive astringent/tonic. Externally, the leaf wash is soothing to tissue redness and inflammation. The root tea is used as a gastrointestinal tract astringent for diarrhea.

There are no cautions for Blackberry. Idaho is also home to Raspberry and Thimbleberry, two other Rubus groupings. Even though Blackberry tends to be a little more seedy than other Rubus fruits, all species are all utilized about the same.

Sustenance Index: Medium
Pictured: *Rubus armeniacus (top & bottom)* | *Rubus ursinus (circle)*

SPRING–SUMMER **SHOOT**

Bracken Fern
Pteridium aquilinum

Other Common Names
Bracken, Western bracken fern, Fiddleneck

Range & Habitat
Widespread throughout the Northern Hemisphere, Bracken fern enjoys a significant distribution in America. In Idaho, the fern is common to montane locations, usually with Ponderosa pine. In fact, deep pine needle chuff and dappled shade seem to reliably point to its presence.

Edible Uses
Late spring to early summer Bracken fern begins to sprout anew from its sub–surface rhizomes. When the stem shoots are 8"–1' in height, snip them at ground level using clippers (or hands alone are fine). Cover the shoots with fresh water and add a teaspoon of baking soda and a teaspoon of salt. Boil/simmer the shoots for about 15 minutes. Drain, rinse, add fresh water (with baking soda and salt), and simmer again for another ten minutes. Drain, rinse, season, and serve as an asparagus–like vegetable.

Medicinal Uses & Cautions
There are no medicinal uses for Bracken fern. Livestock poisonings (and animal studies) leave no doubt that this fern is a harbinger of carcinogenic, mutagenic, and neurotoxic principles (mainly, ptaquiloside). There is even a correlation between higher esophageal cancer rates and Japanese whom regularly consume Bracken fern. With that said, it is my opinion that eating it (boiled with baking soda and salt – this being a Japanese custom, proven to reduce some of its toxicities) **on occasion** is relatively safe. However, eating the fern regularly is probably not wise. I also advise against children and women while pregnant (or nursing) eating Bracken fern. Additionally, intestinal upset is not uncommon if excess is consumed in any one sitting.

Sustenance Index: Low
Pictured: *Pteridium aquilinum*

SPRING–SUMMER | **BULB**

Camas
Camassia quamash

Other Common Names
Small camas, Common camas, Camash, Quamash

Range & Habitat
Pacific Northwest to Inland Northwest is home for Camas. The plant does reach northern Nevada, Utah, and the corner of Wyoming, but just barely. Camas is a meadow–prairie grower, especially if soils are well–hydrated.

Edible Uses
Camas shares many edible aspects with Glacier lily and Mariposa lily. Both are Lily family bulb–type forages.

The bulb: eaten fresh, this part is pleasant tasting, but starchy and mucilaginous. Cooking reduces the starch factor, making it more palatable and also digestible. Wrapping the bulbs with a bouillon cube in foil and letting them cook at the edge of campfire is a simple enough method.

The flower, stem, and leaf: collect and eat these parts early in the season before the plant begins to bolt. They are mild–tasting and fine as salad additions.

Medicinal Uses & Cautions
Camas has no medicinal use nor are there cautions associated with the plant.

Special Note
Camas was an important wild plant–food (and trade item) to nearly all American Indians whom lived in its proximity. Due to its abundance, and low processing labor, the sky was the limit with it as an edible centerpiece: soups, breads, cakes, and so forth.

Be sure of positive identification prior to consuming Camas. A number of poisonous Lily family plants (Deathcamas/Toxicoscordion spp.) may be confused with Camas by the novice. Camas has blue/light blue petals; Deathcamas' petals are cream with green–yellow petal–base spots.

Sustenance Index: High
Pictured: *Camassia quamash*

SUMMER　　　HERBACEOUS PARTS/ROOT

Checkermallow
Sidalcea neomexicana, S. oregana

Other Common Names
Rocky Mountain checkerbloom, Oregon checkerbloom

Range & Habitat
Both species of Checkermallow are found at Ponderosa pine–Fir–Spruce–Aspen elevations. The most reliable areas to look for whatever species are around springs/seeps, moist meadows, and streamsides.

Sidalcea neomexicana is only found in southern parts of the state. S. oregana has the greatest range. It's found nearly state–wide.

Edible Uses
Belonging to the Mallow family, all parts of Checkermallow are mucilaginous (slimy, like Okra) when crushed or chewed. Mild tasting but hairy, the young leaves (and flowers) are well–used as a salad ingredient or pot–herb. Sautéing or steaming the herbal parts tends to reduce the mucilage factor.

The roots of Sidalcea neomexicana are small and semi–tuberous. Pleasant–tasting, crisp, but somewhat mucilaginous, they make a fine fresh edible – wash and eat. They too are good as a cooked item. In terms of usage similarities, Great Plains growing Winecup (Callirhoe involucrata), also in the Mallow family, is a nearly–identical edible plant.

Medicinal Uses, Cautions, & Special Note
Like Marshmallow root, Sidalcea neomexicana's roots, dried and prepared as a tea, are a soothing demulcent/emollient. Checkermallow belongs to the Mallow family – a very safe plant grouping. Sidalcea species are well–known for their leaf dimorphism – shallowly lobed and deeply cleft (upper circle) leaves usually occur on the same plant.

Sustenance Index: Medium
Pictured: *Sidalcea neomexicana*

SPRING | **HERBACEOUS PARTS**

Chickweed
Stellaria media

Other Common Names
Birdweed, Chickenweed, Chick plant

Range & Habitat
A European native, Chickweed is now found nearly worldwide as a cosmopolitan weed. Preferring disturbed soils, look for it around gardens and field edges, trails, park edges, and open woods – really anywhere the soil has at one time been disrupted.

Edible Uses
Chickweed is a simple edible green. Pleasant tasting and mild, it is eaten fresh as potherb/salad addition. If first steamed or sautéed, then as a spinach–like vegetable. It's nothing fancy, nor particularly calorie–dense, however, if a fresh–tasting wild green is on the menu, Chickweed shouldn't disappoint.

Medicinal Uses
Every–other generation Chickweed comes into favor as a diet–aid and general placebo–type healthful herb. At present, I believe we are at the ebb of its medicinal cachet. Poor Chickweed.

But fret not friends! Regardless of claim, Chickweed as a fresh plant poultice is a worthwhile soother of itchy rashes and bites. This is its practical and consistent usage that stands the test of time. Topical preparations made from dried material are usually less active than fresh.

Cautions & Special Note
A very safe plant, Chickweed is caution–free. The related genus, Cerastium, is utilized like Chickweed. Most often referred to as Mouse ear, Idaho is home to several species. They taste about the same as Chickweed, but tend to be less leafy and somewhat fibrous. They too have notched white petals.

Sustenance Index: Low
Pictured: *Stellaria media*

SUMMER | **FRUIT**

Chokecherry
Prunus virginiana var. demissa (P. virginiana var. melanocarpa)

Other Common Names
Western chokecherry

Range & Habitat
The Chokecherry variety in Idaho is var. demissa (sometimes referred to as var. melanocarpa). It's common to the middle mountains, along moist canyon bottoms and just up from streamsides. In the wild, it tends to be a many-stemmed suckering small tree/shrub.

Edible Uses
Chokecherries are edible freshly picked from the tree. When fully ripe (black) they are sweet and have a very pleasant wild cherry flavor (occasionally mildly astringent). Naturally, the pits (seeds) should first be spit out before the fruit is eaten (or removed if processing for jelly or other preparations). Imparting its characteristic flavor, Chokecherry fruit mixes very well with other wild berry combinations.

Bake (important) the pits at 350 degrees for 20 minutes or so. Crack the pit (I use a vise) and eat the kernel within. They are small but pleasant and nutty tasting.

Medicinal Uses, Cautions, & Special Note
The dried bark of Eastern chokecherry (called Wild cherry in the herbal medicine world) is a standard treatment for a dry cough with bronchial inflammation. Western chokecherry is used the same way.

The pits, leaves, and bark contain small amounts of cyanogenic glycosides, common to many Rose family plants. Cooking/heating/drying degrades these compounds. Prior to ripening, Chokecherries are very astringent.

Black cherry (Prunus serotina) is another edible native species of Cherry. It is found further south – AZ, NM, TX, and additionally throughout eastern parts of the country.

Sustenance Index: Medium
Pictured: *Prunus virginiana var. demissa*

SUMMER | **FRUIT**

Currant
Ribes aureum, R. cereum, R. laxiflorum, R. viscosissimum

Other Common Names
Golden currant, Wax currant, Trailing black currant, Sticky currant

Range & Habitat
Like most other inter-mountain western states, Idaho is home to multiple Currant species. Most are medium-sized scraggly bushes and grow at middle elevations.

Edible Uses
Golden currant and Wax currant produce semi-sweet to neutral-tasting berries. Sticky currant with its purple fruit is usually sweeter than the other two. All are fine consumed fresh and also make good jam/jelly candidates. Currant fruit contains fair amounts of vitamin C and health-promoting antioxidant flavonoids.

Medicinal Uses & Cautions
Currant leaves are mildly astringent and used as a fresh poultice for minor scrapes, insect bites, and sunburn. There are no cautious for Currant.

Special Note
Gooseberry is also a Ribes. With a couple of exceptions, Gooseberry types have stem/node thorns. Currant types have no stem/node thorns. Uses for both types are the same. Native species of Currant are related to European Black currant (Ribes nigrum), which is the source of a commercially popular fruit and essential fatty acid supplement (seeds). *See also Gooseberry.*

Ribes hudsonianum (Northern currant) is also found in Idaho. The berries are black and visually appealing, however, more often than not they are bitter/poor tasting. This species is a better jelly candidate rather than a wild forage.

Sustenance Index: Medium
Pictured: *Ribes cereum*

15

SUMMER | **FRUIT**

Elder
Sambucus cerulea (Sambucus glauca, S. neomexicana, S. nigra ssp. cerulea)

Other Common Names
Blue elderberry, Western elder

Range & Habitat
Elder is common to northern Idaho. Further south it's relegated to the higher mountain tops (subalpine) elevations).

Edible Uses
When ripe, Elder berries are blue-black and semi-sweet. Eat them fresh (limited) or dry them for future use. The dried berries can be stored or rehydrated/used as needed. In truth, the drying process concentrates the berries' natural sugars, making them sweeter than fresh. Combine the dried berries with trail mix or eat them as is. The berries are a classic jam/jelly base and can also be fermented instead of grapes to make a wine.

Medicinal Uses & Cautions
The flowers and leaves have similar medicinal uses. Both parts are imbibed as a tea to break a dry fever and as diuretics (the leaves are about twice as strong as the flowers). The tea is also used as a low-level antiviral during the cold and flu season.

Elderberry syrup has a modern following as a cold and flu remedy – this is a recent application with no historical or traditional precedent. If sick, use the flower (or leaf) tea for therapeutic results. Use Elderberry syrup – on pancakes.

The seeds (and other parts of Elder) contain small amounts of sambucine and cyanogenic glycosides. Although these compounds are toxic in larger amounts, eating a small handful of the fresh fruit (with the seed) is not a problem. For the ingestion of larger quantities, the fruit should be heated/dried (which destroys/reduces these compounds) and/or strained of their small seeds (jelly bag).

Sustenance Index: Medium
Pictured: *Sambucus cerulea*

SUMMER | **FRUIT**

Fairybells
Prosartes trachycarpa (Disporum trachycarpum)

Other Common Names
Rough-fruited fairy-bells, Rough-fruited mandarin

Range & Habitat
Fairybells tends to grow at 2000' and higher as an understory herbaceous perennial. Commonly found in the shaded and moist soils of coniferous forests (Pine, Douglas fir, etc.), look for it in the majority of Idaho's mountains.

Edible Uses
Eat the fruit of Fairybells when immature. They are most appealing prior to ripening. At this point they are greenish-white and taste pleasant and cucumber-like. If allowed to fully ripen (reddish-orange) they become poor-tasting and mushy. Fairybells' best use is as a simple trail snack when encountered.

Medicinal Uses
I am unfamiliar with any medicinal use for Fairybells.

Cautions
There are no cautions for Fairybells.

Special Note
Two similar-appearing plants are often found along with Fairybells. Neither are poisonous; however, I cannot fully attest to their palatability.

False Solomon's Seal (Maianthemum racemosum) develops a red berry, but I have found it to be sweet-bitter and unpalatable. Star Solomon's Seal (Maianthemum stellatum) has a green (with blue stripes) berry when immature that turns black when ripe. I have yet to sample Star Solomon's Seal, so am unable to offer an opinion.

Sustenance Index: Medium
Pictured: *Prosartes trachycarpa*

SPRING | HERBACEOUS PARTS

Field Pennycress
Thlaspi arvense

Other Common Names
Fanweed, Frenchweed, Stinkweed

Range & Habitat
Field pennycress is found sporadically in pastures, corral/field edges, grassy berms/ditches, and meadows. It's absent from the higher mountains.

Edible Uses
FP is a Mustard and accordingly, its uses are in-sync with most species in this family. Its closest morphological/usage match is Peppergrass (Lepidium spp.), a well-known, peppery-tasting, Mustard sub-set.

The large fan-shaped seed pods (with pre-formed seeds) are FP's choicest part. They're best collected early-mid spring when tender and flexible. Though a bit fibrous, chopped/puréed they make a nice Mustard-like salad addition or food accent. This part of the plant is the spiciest, so be sure to use it in moderation. The young foliage and flower clusters are used in similar ways, however, these parts do not quite have the same flavorful Mustard-bite as the seedpods.

Medicinal Uses
Eating a small handful of the fresh plant is relieving to indigestion (not heartburn). Most Mustards are mildly diuretic and have been long-used in kidney stone disturbances.

Cautions & Special Note
Large quantities may cause kidney sensitivity and in some women, stimulant menses. The medicinal uses (small amounts) and cautions (large amounts) for this plant are dose-dependent and contingent upon the plant's volatile compounds, mainly comprised of glucosinolates. They too are responsible for FP's sharp-biting-spicy flavor.

Sustenance Index: Low
Pictured: *Thlaspi arvense*

SPRING–SUMMER **BULB**

Glacier Lily
Erythronium grandiflorum

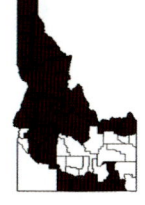

Other Common Names
Avalanche lily, Yellow avalanche lily, Dogtooth fawn lily

Range & Habitat
A plant of the Pacific Northwest and Rocky Mountain regions, look for Glacier lily in and around mountain meadows. Relatedly, in Idaho it's found not in the lowlands, but higher, in the various ranges. Often found in large swaths, its yellow floral display is noteworthy.

Edible Uses
Glacier lily ranks up there with Camas as an important wild food. Utilized by most American Indians whom lived in its proximity, the entire plant is edible. However, the subterranean bulb is the most calorically dense (fortifying) part.

The herbage: fine as a cooked green, this part is most tender early in the season. Later summer it becomes somewhat tough and fibrous. **The bulb:** not far beneath the ground's surface, this is the mostly sought–after part. Once a popular trade item (dried), the bulb is starchy, carbohydrate–dense, and mild–tasting. It is edible fresh, however, a mouthful can be somewhat cloying. Better first steamed or baked, heat application tends to improve the bulb's texture and renders it more digestible.

Medicinal Uses & Cautions
There are no medicinal uses or cautions for Glacier lily.

Special Note
Glacier lily joins Camas, Mariposa lily, and Yellow fritillary as a group of edible Lily family bulbs. If one species is not abundant, that's alright, just find another; they're all very similar in edible aspects.

Sustenance Index: High
Pictured: *Erythronium grandiflorum*

SUMMER | FRUIT

Gooseberry
Ribes inerme, R. lacustre, R. montigenum, R. niveum, R. oxyacanthoides, R. velutinum

Other Common Names
Whitestem gooseberry, Black gooseberry, Mountain gooseberry, Snowy gooseberry, Canadian gooseberry, Desert gooseberry

Range & Habitat
Idaho is home to six species of Gooseberry. They vary to some degree in distribution, however, the surest habitats for these bushes are middle mountain open coniferous forests and forest edges.

Edible Uses
Gooseberries are the size of a small grape/large pea and purple–black when fully ripe. They are fine consumed fresh; also, they make a serviceable jelly base or can be dried and rehydrated for future use. Their seeds are small enough to be eaten unnoticed. Additionally, like most Ribes berries, Gooseberry is high in vitamin C.

Most black–fruited Ribes (both Currant and Gooseberry) species in Idaho tend to be sweeter than red–fruited ones. However, Ribes hudsonianum (Northern currant), tends to be bitter and R. niveum (Snowy gooseberry), sour.

Medicinal Uses & Cautions
Like Currant, Gooseberry leaf is a mild astringent and is used as a topical soother for minor sunburn, scrapes, and abrasions. There are no cautions for Gooseberry.

Special Note
Ribes species are loosely separated into one of two groups by whether or not they have stem/node thorns. If the plant is spiny, then it is a Gooseberry. If the plant is spineless, then it is a Currant. Aside from slight botanical differences, edible (and medicinal) uses for both types are the same.

Sustenance Index: Medium
Pictured: *Ribes inerme (top & circle)* | *Ribes leptanthum (bottom)*

SUMMER | **FRUIT**

Hawthorn
Crataegus spp.

Other Common Names
Fireberry Hawthorn, Black hawthorn, Huckleberry hawthorn, River hawthorn, and so forth

Range & Habitat
Hawthorn is a small tree with toothed leaves, 5-petaled white flowers, thorns, and red (occasionally purple-black, depending on species) fruit. The most commonly found species in Idaho is Crataegus douglasii (Black hawthorn). It's found throughout the central-northern parts of the state. For whatever species, it's generally found along stream and canyon sides and on slopes/hillsides just up from ponds/lakes/reservoirs.

Edible Uses
Ripening mid-late summer, Hawthorn berries are sweet to neutral but seed-filled. Aside from mouthing a few berries at a time (and spitting out the seeds), the fruit's best use is as a jelly base. The berries are rich in vitamin C, B vitamins, and various antioxidants.

Medicinal Uses
Although Hawthorn can be thought of as being edible, it's really the plant's medicinal quality that stands out. The fruit, flowers, and young leaves are a time-honored cardiovascular medicine. Colorado's species are similar in use to the better known European species; that is, herbal preparations of Hawthorn are extensively-researched and well-tolerated. They are effectively applied towards low-level (pre-surgical intervention) heart complaints. High blood pressure and poor valvular function are two main indications that point to Hawthorn's use.

Cautions & Special Note
Hawthorn in caution-free. It is related to Rose (Rose hips), Serviceberry, and Raspberry.

Sustenance Index: Medium
Pictured: *Crataegus rivularis*

21

SUMMER | **FRUIT**

Hollygrape
Berberis aquifolium, B. nervosa, B. repens

Other Common Names
Oregongrape, Cascade oregongrape, Creeping hollygrape

Range & Habitat
Three species of Hollygrape are found in Idaho. They are semi-shade oriented small to medium-sized perennials apt to grow in association with conifers – Pine, Fir, Doug-Fir, etc.

Edible Uses
Ripening from middle to late summer, the small, blue, bloom-covered fruit develop from 6-petaled cup-shaped yellow flowers.

The berries form in clutches and are pleasant tasting: sweet-tart with a hint of bitter. They are fine consumed fresh or can be prepared as a jelly/fruit preserve. Another option is to dehydrate the berries and add them to trail mix and the like.

Medicinal Uses
Hollygrape (all species) is of medicinal import. The roots contain isoquinoline alkaloids (berberine, et al.) making them useful in treating an array of liver, gastrointestinal, and microbial complaints. Most herbalists (worldwide) utilize various species of Berberis in some capacity. *See Medicinal Plants of the Western Mountain States for a full write-up.*

Cautions
There are no cautions for the fruit.

Special Note
A related plant, Barberry (Berberis vulgaris), is found occasionally as an ornamental and/or escapee in Idaho. It has stem thorns (verses Hollygrape's spiny leaves) are red fruit. Hollygrape and Barberry are closely related. All have edible berries and similar medicinal uses.

Sustenance Index: Medium
Pictured: *Berberis aquifolium (top) | B. repens (bottom)*

SUMMER | **FRUIT**

Huckleberry
Vaccinium membranaceum, V. caespitosum, V. myrtillus, V. scoparium

Other Common Names
Thinleaf huckleberry, Dwarf bilberry, Whortleberry, Grouse whortleberry

Range & Habitat
Four Vaccinium species are found in Idaho, with Huckleberry and Bilberry being the most common. For whatever species, the names Huckleberry, Bilberry, and Whortleberry are loosely interchangeable. All are Blueberry type plants of the Heath family.

Huckleberry and the others are found in montane/subalpine regions throughout the Rockies (and Pacific Northwest). Associating with conifers, slopes, hillsides, and drainage sides are some of their usual areas.

Edible Uses
Although Blueberry (Vaccinium corymbosum) has a larger fruit, consider Huckleberry (and others) identical in all edible aspects. A summertime berry, look closely for the fruit among the leaves. They are delicious eaten fresh. Additionally, its utility as a dried berry or prepared as a jelly, preserve, or syrup needs little explanation.

As for the fruit's nutritional value, it contains fair amounts of vitamins A, C, and a number of B vitamins. Potassium, magnesium, and calcium are additionally listed for the fruit.

Medicinal Uses & Cautions
Bilberry fruit extract (Vaccinium myrtillus) has a well–established following as an ocular preventive medicine. It's mostly employed as an antioxidant to slow the progression of cataracts, macular degeneration, and related eye disturbances. Bilberry leaf tea is mildly astringent and traditionally used to counter diarrhea and reduce renal irritation. Other Vaccinium species have similar medicinal effects. There are no cautions for Huckleberry, et al.

Sustenance Index: Medium
Pictured: *Vaccinium membranaceum*

SPRING-SUMMER — **SEED**

Indian Rice Grass
Achnatherum hymenoides (Oryzopsis hymenoides, Stipa hymenoides)

Other Common Names
Indian mountain ricegrass, Indian millet, Silky mountain rice

Range & Habitat
A native bunch grass, Indian rice grass is fairly common throughout Idaho. Well-drained and sun-exposed hillsides, slopes, and flats are some of its ideal locations.

Edible Uses
The seed is gathered from late spring through early fall – lower elevation plants flower/fruit earlier than higher elevation ones. Lightly pinch with thumb and forefinger below a fruiting panicle; then gently pull, stripping the seed away from the stem.

Place the seed in a paper bag and repeat. Set the seed aside for 1–2 weeks so it dries completely. One de-chaffing technique for small amounts is to simply rub a bunch between hands several feet above a container in a light breeze (or a fan set on low). Slowly let the seed/chaff fall. The breeze will take away the chaff while the heavier seed drops into the container. Keep repeating this process until only the grain remains.

Another way is to parch the seed, so the fuzzy chaff is burnt away (bottom photo). Prepare Indian rice grass like any other seed/grain: cooked whole, as a flour or meal, etc.

Medicinal Uses & Cautions
There are no medicinal uses/cautions for Indian rice grass.

Special Note
Before corn arrived on the scene, the plant was a main grain staple of the western Indians. The plant's commonality and seed size (for a native grass, it's one of the largest) made it a valuable and much utilized edible.

Sustenance Index: High
Pictured: *Achnatherum hymenoides*

SPRING–SUMMER | **HERBACEOUS PARTS/SEED**

Lambsquarters
Chenopodium album var. album

Other Common Names
Goosefoot, Quelites, Chual

Range & Habitat
Lambsquarters is common throughout Idaho. It's non-native and weedy in habit, so does well in disturbed soils: roadsides, trailsides, grassy areas, field margins, etc.

Edible Uses
The plant's young leaves are the most palatable part; with age they often become a little acrid. For the consumption of moderate to large quantities, the leaves should first be boiled, then rinsed. Most species are high in calcium and vitamin A. The seeds of Lambsquarters (related to Amaranth) too are a good food source. They are gathered and winnowed once the plant starts to bolt; after which they are ground into a meal or simply added to and/or cooked with other foods.

Medicinal Uses
Epazote (Chenopodium [Dysphania] ambrosioides) is the main medicinal species of the genus. It is not found in the wild (Idaho), but it can be cultivated in the garden. A spice and useful carminative, Epazote also smells and tastes differently than Lambsquarters: when crushed fresh, like restroom disinfectant.

Cautions & Special Note
Kidney stone suffers may find that eating large amounts of the fresh plant (daily) will contribute to this condition (due to a high oxalate content). There is no problem with Lambsquarters as an occasional edible. Chenopodium album is the main edible Lambsquarters species. It is common in Idaho. However, Chenopodium fremontii (bottom pic) is also abundant in southern parts of the state. They both have identical edible uses. Generally, wider-leaf species are more palatable than thin-leaf species.

Sustenance Index: Medium
Pictured: *Chenopodium album* (top) | *C. fremontii* (bottom)

SPRING–SUMMER | **LEAF**

Mallow
Malva neglecta

Other Common Names
Common mallow, Cheeseweed, Cheeseplant

Range & Habitat
Two species of Mallow are found in Idaho, but only Malva neglecta is distributed with any frequency. A people/animal plant, Mallow will almost always be found in disturbed soils: dirt roadsides, walkway edges, old grades, fallow fields, pastures, etc. Like most annual herbs, it grows aggressively in response to warmer–season rains.

Edible Uses
The young leaves, being the most palatable part, are simply eaten raw or mixed with other greens as a salad. Really though, they are better boiled or steamed. With added butter and seasoning, most find them similar to cooked spinach. They'll be a little mucilaginous/slimy (Mallow is related to Okra), but still mild tasting and nutritious.

Although the leaf tea does have some medicinal application, it is pleasant enough to be used as a beverage.

Medicinal Uses
The leaves make a soothing tea for sore throats and coughs. Drink it throughout the day if suffering from a cold or flu. This will also assist with hydration and mildly stimulate innate immunity, due to the plant's arabinogalactan content.

Cautions & Special Note
There are no cautions for Mallow. Mallow is closely related to Checkermallow (Sidalcea). In fact, both species should be treated the same in terms of edibility (herbaceous parts).

Sustenance Index: Low
Pictured: *Malva neglecta*

SPRING | **SAMARA**

Maple
Acer glabrum, A. grandidentatum, A. negundo

Other Common Names
Rocky Mountain maple, Bigtooth maple, Ash–leaf maple, Box elder

Range & Habitat
Three species of Acer are common in Idaho. Rocky Mountain maple and Bigtooth maple are usually found at higher elevations; Box elder, somewhat lower. They all prefer rich–moist soils in proximity to streams/drainages.

Edible Uses
A simple trail–forage or pot herb, the very young samaras (winged fruit) are the sought–after item. Eaten as–is they have a not–too coarse texture and neutral taste (sometimes a little bitter). The samaras are fine added to salads and/or prepared/seasoned as a cooked green. They are edible for only 1–2 weeks in the spring when immature and greenish (sometimes reddish). Later in the season, they become fibrous and bitter.

Although often cited as an edible part, the maturing seed (bottom pic) of whatever Maple species is often more bitter than not. But no harm will come to the consumer by sampling this part (first remove the seed from the fibrous wing). If fair/pleasant tasting, maybe you've discovered the mythical patch of good–tasting Maple seed!

Medicinal Uses & Cautions
There are no significant medicinal uses or cautions for Maple.

Special Note
Broadly speaking any Maple species, not just Sugar Maple (Acer saccharum), is a potential source of Maple syrup (or rather Maple sap). The main determining factor is winter temperatures. If temperatures are sub–freezing at night and less than lower 40s throughout the day, then it's worth a try.

Sustenance Index: Low
Pictured: *Acer negundo* (top) | *Acer grandidentatum* (bottom)

SPRING–SUMMER | **HERBACEOUS PARTS/BULB**

Mariposa Lily
Calochortus elegans, C. eurycarpus, C. macrocarpus, C. nuttallii, and so forth

Other Common Names
Fringed mariposa lily, White mariposa lily, Sagebrush mariposa lily, Sego lily

Range & Habitat
The epicenter of the Calochortus genus is California where dozens of species exist. In Idaho, eight species are listed, but only four are relatively abundant. Although elevations tend to vary depending on species, Mariposa lily prefers full sun and sandy–rocky soils. Look for these plants on slopes, gradual hillsides, and flats.

Edible Uses
From flower and stem to root bulb, all parts of Mariposa lily are edible. The buds, flowers, young seed pods, stems, and leaves are eaten without killing the plant. These parts are pleasant tasting and have a mild nutty flavor.

The bulbs require slightly more effort to procure. They are often ½' or so beneath the ground's surface, so digging with a trowel is necessary. The bulbs provide more sustenance than the upper parts due to their greater carbohydrate content. They are pleasant tasting (but starchy). Eat them raw or cooked.

Medicinal Uses & Cautions
Mariposa lily has no medicinal use nor are there cautions associated with the plant.

Special Note
Be sure the population at hand is abundant. Two Idaho species (Calochortus gunnisonii and C. nitidus) are limited in distribution.

All species are only identifiable for 2–4 weeks when in flower/seed. After this window has passed, its above–ground trace is gone until next year.

Sustenance Index: High
Pictured: *Calochortus nuttallii*

SPRING | **HERBACEOUS PARTS**

Miner's Lettuce
Claytonia perfoliata

Other Common Names
Indian lettuce, Winter purslane, Spring beauty

Range & Habitat
Miner's lettuce is a common western US annual. In Idaho, it is surprising variable in elevation requirement, being found mostly below 8000'.

Needing shady and damp soils to thrive, in early–mid spring, look for the plant next to streams, among rocks and boulders, and in dappled shade from Maple, Juniper, Balsam poplar, and Ponderosa pine.

Edible Uses
All above–ground parts of Miner's lettuce are edible. Mildly tart and succulent, it is a most–refreshing wild forage. Simply eat the foliage alone or add Miner's lettuce to salads or use it as a garnish. Although still edible, once cooked/boiled Miner's lettuce loses much of its taste and appeal.

Medicinal Uses & Cautions
There are no medicinal uses for Miner's lettuce.

If eating large amounts everyday, a quick simmer of the leaf should first be employed. Compounds (oxalates), common to most Purslane family plants, can irritate the kidneys (kidney stone suffers may want to eat Miner's lettuce sparingly).

Special Note
Western spring beauty and Bitterroot are Miner's lettuce's closest associates. Foliage uses for all plants are the same; however, unlike the other two, Miner's lettuce has an insignificant root system. Accordingly, that portion is not particularly edible. The plant fades very quickly as Spring progresses, so it is available for only 2–3 weeks early in the season.

Sustenance Index: Low
Pictured: *Claytonia perfoliata*

SPRING | **LEAF**

Monkey Flower
Mimulus guttatus

Other Common Names
Yellow monkey flower, Common monkey flower, Seep monkey flower

Range & Habitat
Over a dozen species of Monkey flower are found in Idaho. However, only one species is common (and palatable) enough to be considered here. Found throughout a surprising array of elevations, look for Monkey flower around (or directly in) water. Creeks, springs, and seeps reliably host the plant – lake/pond sides, not so much.

Entirely a plant of western North America, Monkey flower is absent from the Plains and eastward.

Edible Uses
Monkey flower makes for a fair-tasting early springtime green. The young leaves, before the plant's stem and flowers develop, is the choice edible part. At this time, the leaves are eaten raw, or boiled/steamed and consumed as a cooked green. Their taste is like mildly bitter lettuce.

Further along in the season, when Monkey flower becomes a mature plant, it can still be eaten raw, but is often too bitter to be consumed in any quantity. Boiling the leaf, then following up with a quick rinse will remove some of its bitterness, allowing greater amounts to be ingested.

Medicinal Uses, Cautions, & Special Note
The mature leaf as a tea is a simple bitter tonic. Use it to assist digestion as a pre-meal beverage. There are no cautions for Monkey flower. The plant may be confused with Watercress when young and not in flower (they both grow in water). Taste a leaf. If bland yet a little bitter, it is Monkey flower; if mustard-spicy, then Watercress. Mimulus glabratus (Roundleaf monkey flower) is an occasional species in Utah. It grows in similar habitats; however, it is smaller and generally prostrate. It is utilized like Mimulus guttatus.

Sustenance Index: Low
Pictured: *Mimulus guttatus*

SUMMER | **FRUIT**

Mulberry
Morus alba

Other Common Names
White mulberry, Russian mulberry, Silkworm mulberry

Range & Habitat
Native to east Asia, Mulberry has been widely planted throughout the country as an ornamental shade tree with edible fruit. Most populations tend to be older plantings as property markers, hedgerows, or simply shade/yard trees.

It's likely that some individual trees have become naturalized – seeds spread by birds/animals. Escapees are almost always found in association with bottomlands, streamsides, and forest margins next to roads, fields, and other open areas.

Edible Uses
Mulberry fruit are a well-known edible. When ripe (purple to dark red) they are sweet and juicy and best eaten when picked fresh from the tree. They can also be prepared as a jelly, preserve, or simply dried and added to snack foods. The purple fruit have the highest anthocyanin content – health-promoting antioxidant pigments. They are also a fair source of potassium and vitamin C.

Cautions & Medicinal Uses
There are no cautions (nor significant medicinal uses) for Mulberry.

Special Note
Two native species of Mulberry grow east of California. Texas mulberry (Morus microphylla) is found throughout the Southwest. Red mulberry (M. rubra) is very similar in appearance to White mulberry and is found in central/eastern parts of the country. Both plants also have edible fruit. Fig tree (Ficus spp.) is also in the Mulberry family (Moraceae), as is Breadfruit (Artocarpus altilis) and Jackfruit (A. heterophyllus). The leaf of Morus alba is the primary natural food of the silkworm.

Sustenance Index: Medium
Pictured: *Morus alba*

| SUMMER | STEM |

Mullein
Verbascum thapsus

Other Common Names
Woolly mullein, Gordolobo

Range & Habitat
Mullein is a biannual, non-native weed. Exceedingly common to Ponderosa pine elevations, it's found almost always in disturbed soils – roadsides, trailsides, and fire-swept areas.

Edible Uses
Early to mid-summer select a second-year plant. Clip the last 8"–12" of flexible flowering stalk and carefully remove the adhering flower buds and outer rough layer. What's left will be a tender and pliable inner stem, somewhat thinner than a pencil. Eat this part raw or once cooked and seasoned. Having an asparagus-like taste and texture, use it as a dish by itself or in combination with other wild foods. Given that entire mountain sides (after a fire) are often covered by hundreds of plants, Mullein is an often over-looked but plentiful edible plant.

Medicinal Uses, Cautions, & Special Note
Mullein leaf tea (well-strained) is a standard herbal treatment for a dry hacky cough. The root is used for urinary irritations, and the flower, prepared as an oil, is a soothing earache treatment.

For Mullein's edible use there are no cautions. It's occasionally referred to as 'toilet-paper plant' by campers due to its leaf size and softness. Proceed at your own risk...itchy! Relatedly, internet sources (sigh) suggest applying the whole leaf as a topical treatment for diaper rash, skin inflammations, etc. Mullein's stellate hairs will likely exasperate these types of problems. Think fiber glass: at first feels like cotton candy, but then later...

First-year Mullein maintains a form as a basal rosette of leaves. During its second year, the plant produces a 3'–5' tall flowering stalk (then dies).

Sustenance Index: Medium
Pictured: *Verbascum thapsus*

SPRING–SUMMER **HERBACEOUS PARTS**

Nettle
Urtica dioica ssp. gracilis, U. dioica ssp. holosericea

Other Common Names
Stinging nettle, California nettle

Range & Habitat
Two subspecies (one species) of Nettle are found in Idaho. Both subspecies are generally encountered in moist soils, around streams and drainages, with conifers (usually Douglas fir).

Edible Uses
The ideal time to gather Nettle for food is when it is first forming in the spring, prior to the plant becoming fibrous and coarse. It is important to simmer/boil Nettle for 5–10 minutes, sometimes longer depending on the plant's maturity. This softens the herb and renders the stinging hairs inert.

Once boiled, Nettle has the consistency of most other cooked wild greens. It is non–bitter and nutrient–dense.

Medicinal Uses
Nettle leaf tea is a mineral–rich and alkalizing beverage. The tea is also soothing to urinary irritations and calming to rhinitis/hayfever.

Cautions
Wear gloves/long sleeves when collecting Nettle due to the plant's stinging hairs (trichomes). If stung, the weal (welt) subsides in 30–60 minutes; nevertheless, it is mildly to moderately painful. If Nettle greens are not cooked sufficiently some mouth/throat irritation may occur from improperly neutralized trichomes.

Special Note
Prior to Cotton's dominance, Nettle's fibrous stems (similar to Hemp) were once a base material for cloths, tents, bags, etc.

Sustenance Index: Low
Pictured: *Urtica dioica ssp. gracilis*

SUMMER | **LEAF/SEED**

Orach
Atriplex hortensis, A. micrantha, A. rosea

Other Common Names
Garden orach, Russian orach, Tumbling orach

Range & Habitat
Generally, the Orach species of Atriplex are annual, fast-growing, leafy, and non-native (Eurasia). Idaho is home to several such plants, with Atriplex rosea (Tumbling orach) being the most common.

Look for these plants in ditches, next to culverts, edges of secondary roadsides, and similar moist/disturbed soils. They germinate and grow quickly in response to seasonal rains.

Edible Uses
Related to Amaranth and Lambsquarters, botanically and in use, consider Orach a low-level edible. The young/just-forming leaves are eaten fresh in small amounts. However, they are best simmered/rinsed and consumed as a spinach-like vegetable. I've yet to sample the seeds, but it is said they are somewhat edible and similar to what Lambsquarters' provides.

Medicinal Uses
There are no medicinal uses for Orach.

Cautions
Most species of Atriplex harbor moderate to high levels of oxalates; accordingly, be sure to simmer/rinse the leaves before eating large amounts.

Special Note
The perennial species of Atriplex are generally referred to as Saltbush. These plants tend to accumulate sodium, particularly on leaf surfaces. Inversely, most Orach types are not especially salty.

Sustenance Index: Low
Pictured: *Atriplex rosea*

SUMMER | **LEAF**

Ox-Eye Daisy
Leucanthemum vulgare

Other Common Names
Great ox-eye, Field daisy, Maudlin daisy

Range & Habitat
An abundant Rocky Mountain non-native weed, Ox-eye daisy grows in and around the majority of Idaho's ranges. Look for the plant along dirt roadsides, forest edges, and in open meadows. It prefers full sun exposures.

Edible Uses
Gather the basal leaves early in the season before the plant develops a flowering stalk. At this point they will be slightly thickened and tender. Fresh, they have a mild taste and are fine used as a garnish or salad addition. Larger amounts should be boiled/sautéed and seasoned accordingly. Ox-eye daisy's caloric content (low) is similar to other leafy greens, so it should be thought of as an addition or garnish food, and not as a main course.

Medicinal Uses
The dried upper herb (flower and leaf), prepared as a tea is a mild child-safe sudorific/sedative, similar to Chamomile in effect.

Cautions
There are no cautions for Ox-eye daily.

Special Note
A number of other Leucanthemum/Chrysanthemum species (i.e. Chrysanthemum cinerariaefolium or Dalmatian daisy) contain pyrethrins, a group of naturally occurring compounds with well-documented insecticidal properties. These compounds also tend to be mildly to moderately toxic when ingested in sufficient quantities. There are no consistent reports of Ox-eye daisy containing these compounds, at least in greater than trace amounts.

Sustenance Index: Low
Pictured: *Leucanthemum vulgare*

SUMMER | **SEED**

Panicgrass
Panicum capillare

Other Common Names
Common panicgrass, Witchgrass, Ticklegrass, Tumble panic

Range & Habitat
A widespread North American annual grass, Panicum capillare is the most commonly encountered species in Idaho.

It's a plant of middle elevations and needs moist/disturbed soils to thrive. Look for it around ditches, dirt roadsides, dam and reservoir areas, and field edges.

Edible Uses
Snip the entire panicle (with 2"–3" of stem) from the grass in late August – too soon and the seeds will not be mature; too late and they will have fallen.

Place the panicles in a paper bag and set them aside for about a week. Strip the seeds from the stems by pinching low on the bunch and pulling towards the top. And/or the panicles can be rolled between the hands. Give the seeds (and small stems) a vigorous hand–rubbing and then winnow them in a light breeze (or fan set on low). Panicgrass is small enough to be eaten unprocessed, so enjoy the whole seed (crunchy–mildly nutty) solo, or sprinkled on salads, meat, etc. They too are fine for flour/meal/gruel/sun–dried cakes. The flour was commonly mixed with acorn meal, cornmeal, and/or Indian rice grass seed flour. Nutritious, the seed contains good amounts of protein, carbohydrates, and fats.

Medicinal Uses, Cautions, & Special Note
There are no medicinal uses or cautions for Panicgrass. Like most Panicum species, this plant provided an important nutritional source in primitive times.

Sustenance Index: High
Pictured: *Panicum capillare*

SPRING–SUMMER — **HERBACEOUS PARTS**

Pellitory
Parietaria pensylvanica

Other Common Names
Pennsylvania pellitory

Range & Habitat
Like most other Parietaria species, Pennsylvania pellitory is an annual small forb/herb. It tends to do well in sheltered areas – next to boulders and thickets, in rock crevices, and under shade–providing shrubs and trees (low to middle elevations). It bolts quickly as temperatures rise.

Edible Uses
Gather the tender young leaves/stems as a simple forage/pot herb. These parts are a little hairy, but nevertheless, pleasant as a green. Fresh, Pellitory's taste is distinctly cucumber–like and similar to Chickweed.

The herb too is fine cooked/sautéed. In this form it's close to Nettle in taste/texture. Also in most nutritional aspects, Pellitory is similar to Nettle.

Medicinal Uses
Its closest useful relative is Parietaria officinalis or Pellitory–of–the–wall, a European native often used medicinally like Nettle (Urtica dioica). Both Pellitory–of–the–wall and Nettle are useful in treating acidic conditions such as gout and urate–type kidney stones/deposits. They also are fair–tasting and used as simple beverage teas.

Cautions
Other Parietaria species are considered problematic allergen–producers (pollen). It's unknown whether or not the regional species is problematic.

Sustenance Index: Low
Pictured: *Parietaria pensylvanica*

SPRING–SUMMER | **LEAF**

Plantain
Plantago major

Other Common Names
Common plantain, Lanté

Range & Habitat
Plantain is a non-native short-lived perennial. Look for the plant in moist and disturbed soils such as trailsides, meadows, and streamsides (and even untended lawns). Generally abundant, it's a plant that is encountered with little searching.

Edible Uses
Plantain is entirely edible, yet the young springtime leaves are the choice part. They can be eaten fresh, but most find them better as a cooked green. Sautéed, boiled, or steamed, the leaves are fair-tasting and can be eaten alone, or added to other wild food preparations.

Medicinal Uses
A mild plant medicine, Plantain is simply used topically as a soothing vulnerary. Internally, as a tea or fresh juice, it is antiinflammatory and healing to gastrointestinal ulcerations.

Cautions
There are no cautions for Plantain.

Special Note
All other species of Plantain are edible (or at least not poisonous), though this species is considered one of the most palatable. Psyllium fiber, a common over-the-counter dietary supplement, is derived from the seed/seed husk of Plantago ovata. Plantain is unrelated to the cooking type of plantain (Musa spp.). The latter is a type of banana that is often used in Mexican cuisine.

Sustenance Index: Low
Pictured: *Plantago major*

38

SUMMER | **FRUIT**

Raspberry
Rubus idaeus ssp. strigosus

Other Common Names
Red raspberry, American red raspberry, Western red raspberry

Range & Habitat
Raspberry is a common Rocky Mountain understory herbaceous shrub. It's found throughout all the higher mountains of Idaho. Associated with Fir, Spruce, and Aspen, look to creek and drainage sides, canyon bottoms, and moist slopes and hills.

Edible Uses
Raspberry fruit found in the wild tends to be a little smaller than store-bought cultivars; however, at peak ripeness they are just as sweet, possibly even more so. They are fine consumed fresh and can too be utilized as a preserve or jelly base. In all ways, consider wild Raspberry identical in use to the fruit found in commerce.

Relatively high in vitamin C, the fruit contains approximately 30 milligrams per 8 ounces. It also is a far source of a number of B vitamins and vitamin E.

Medicinal Uses
Raspberry leaf tea is a female reproductive tonic mainly used throughout the last trimester of pregnancy. The tea is also soothing to urinary tract irritations.

Cautions
There are no cautions for Raspberry.

Special Note
Rubus leucodermis (Black raspberry) is found occasionally in central parts of the state. Its fruits are black when ripe, but just as tastily as the common species. Raspberry is closely related to Thimbleberry, Dewberry, Blackberry, and Salmonberry (all Rubus species). American and East Asian Raspberry is Rubus idaeus ssp. strigosus. Store bought Raspberries are from cultivars of European raspberry (Rubus idaeus ssp. idaeus).

Sustenance Index: Medium
Pictured: *Rubus idaeus ssp. strigosus*

FALL | **FRUIT**

Russian Olive
Elaeagnus angustifolia

Other Common Names
Silver Berry, Oleaster, Wild olive

Range & Habitat
Native to Asia, Russian olive is abundantly found as an exotic throughout the inter-mountain western states. Considered invasive, it's almost always found next to waterways, rivers, and related bottomlands.

Edible Uses
I'm not a big fan of Russian olive as a wild edible. It has too high of a tannin content for my taste. However, if you decide to proceed, it's important to allow the fruit to fully ripen on the tree prior to collection. If picked too soon, the fruit is very astringent and essentially inedible. Pay attention to the fruit around early fall/first frost. Gather them just before to dropping to the ground. At this point they can be eaten raw in limited amounts. They'll still be somewhat astringent and mealy, but slightly sweet too. However, in order to consume them in any quantity, they'll need to be water-leached.

Submerge the fruit in water, changing it daily until the fruit are astringency-free. Once relatively free of tannins, a seasoning brine is added. This is similar to traditional raw olive processing.

Once roasted, the seed of Russian olive is edible as well. It's best ground into a meal and added to other flours in baking.

Medicinal Uses, Cautions, & Special Note
The powdered dried fruit mixed with a beverage is a traditional diarrhea remedy. This is due to the berry's abundance of tannins. Relatedly, too much will cause constipation. Russian olive is closely related to Autumn olive, a more edible Wild olive species (Elaeagnus umbellata).

Sustenance Index: Low
Pictured: *Elaeagnus angustifolia*

SPRING–SUMMER | **ENTIRE PLANT**

Salsify
Tragopogon dubius, T. porrifolius, T. pratensis

Other Common Names
Yellow salsify, Goat's beard, Oyster root, Purple salsify, Meadow salsify

Range & Habitat
The three most common Idaho Salsify species are non–native and originally from Europe. They do well at middle elevations, particularly in grassy areas that have at one time been disturbed – lawn and park edges, trailsides, embankments, etc.

    Tragopogon dubius (Yellow salsify) is by far the most regularly encountered species (yellow flowers). It's found statewide.

Edible Uses
The upper parts (flower, leaf, and stem) are picked and eaten raw, or steamed/sautéed as a cooked green. A good tasting and mild plant, the above–ground parts are non–bitter and very palatable. Try to collect the foliage before the flower goes to seed. It is more tender at this point.

    Salsify roots can be eaten raw, but most find them better if first boiled/steamed/sautéed. They are mildly bitter–tasting (I don't think they taste like oysters) and provide more complex carbohydrates than the upper parts. The roots of older plants tend to be more fibrous and bitter, especially if in their second or third year.

Medicinal Uses & Cautions
There are no significant medicinal uses or cautions for Salsify.

Special Note
All parts of the plant exude a milky latex if cut or torn. Another identifying feature is its large softball–sized seed puff–ball.

Sustenance Index: Medium
Pictured: *Tragopogon dubius*

SUMMER **FRUIT**

Serviceberry
Amelanchier alnifolia, A. cusickii, A. utahensis

Other Common Names
Alder–leaf serviceberry, Cusick's shadbush, Utah serviceberry

Range & Habitat
Serviceberry is primarily a shrub of the Rocky Mountains (and Pacific–States). Idaho hosts three species: Amelanchier alnifolia (Alder–leaf serviceberry), A. cusickii (Cusick's shadbush) and A. utahensis (Utah serviceberry).

Look for whichever species on rocky hillsides and slopes, with a stream or drainage not far away. Ponderosa pine and Juniper are usual companion trees.

Edible Uses
Ripening mid to late summer, the purple fruit are eaten raw. If found in optimal condition they are sweet and juicy – truly a delight. Once dehydrated the berries too are a fine addition to trail mix and dried fruit combos. Of course Serviceberry is a great item as a jelly, preserve, or a similar preparation.

Like other dark–pigmented fruits, the berries are filled with health–promoting anthrocyanins (ck).

Medicinal Uses
Aside from the leaves' mild astringency, there are no medicinal uses for Serviceberry.

Cautions
Like most from the Rose family, Serviceberry seed (very small), contains traces of cyanogenic glycosides. However, fear not, it is virtually impossible to consume the volume of berries needed to produce symptoms. Drying/heating the seed destroys these compounds.

Sustenance Index: Medium
Pictured: *Amelanchier utahensis (top)* | *Amelanchier alnifolia (circle & bottom)*

42

SPRING–SUMMER — **LEAF**

Sheep's Sorrel
Rumex acetosella

Other Common Names
Field sorrel, Red sorrel

Range & Habitat
This non–native little herbaceous perennial is somewhat common to middle–higher elevations. Preferring disturbed soils, look for it next to trails, ditches, and minimally–traveled dirt roadsides in full sun exposures.

Edible Uses
Sheep's sorrel is best utilized as a fresh herb in salads or as a garnish. The leaves being the main edible part, are tangy and sour-tasting (oxalates). Moderate amounts can be consumed raw; however, if eating more than a hand-full, I recommend first giving the leaves a quick boil and rinse. This will diminish some of the leaves' oxalate content.

Medicinal Uses
Sheep's sorrel is not particularly medicinal; however, the plant's therapeutic void has not stopped product hucksters from promoting it as part of a 'cancer–cure' herbal combination.

Cautions
Excess consumption of oxalates may lead to urinary tract irritation and stone development (if prone to their formation). Boiling/rinsing Sheep's sorrel reduces its oxalate concentration.

Special Note
Two characteristics will help in identifying Sheep's sorrel: 1) sour taste; 2) the leaves are arrow–shaped with pointed base lobes (hastate). Sheep's sorrel and Yellowdock are closely related (both are Rumex). Sheep's sorrel is best as a fresh garnish. Yellowdock is better as a cooked green.

Sustenance Index: Low
Pictured: *Rumex acetosella*

SPRING–SUMMER — **LEAF**

Sow Thistle
Sonchus spp.

Other Common Names
Common sow thistle, Spiny sow thistle

Range & Habitat
A weedy non-native annual, look for Sow thistle in moistened-disturbed soils and around rocky draws that run with intermittent water. Wild lettuce (Lactuca), a plant that is similar in appearance, botanical relation, and edible use, is often found growing near Sow thistle.

Edible Uses
Collect Sow thistle's young leaves when the plant first emerges as a basal rosette in the spring. They are best cooked: boiling, sautéing, or steaming will soften the leaf spines on at least one species (Sonchus asper). Boiling and rinsing the leaves with fresh water will lessen their bitterness.

Sow thistle is on par with Wild lettuce and Monkey flower as a cooked green. It may not be the best wild edible, but it works well to round out some of the better tasting cacti fruit and legumes.

Medicinal Uses
Sow thistle leaf tea is sometimes used as a Dandelion leaf substitute.

Cautions
There are no cautions for Sow thistle.

Special Note
Like Dandelion and Wild lettuce, Sow thistle has a milky sap when a leaf is broken.

Sustenance Index: Low
Pictured: *Sonchus oleraceus* (top) | *Sonchus asper* (bottom)

SPRING–SUMMER | **ENTIRE PLANT**

Springparsley
Cymopterus glaucus, C. glomeratus C. terebinthinus, and so forth

Other Common Names
Waxy springparsley, Fendler's springparsley (Chimaja), Turpentine springparsley

Range & Habitat
Idaho is home to 12 species of Springparsley, half of which are found infrequently (or rarely). The other six are abundant enough to gather when encountered. They thrive at middle elevations: dry basins, slopes, and rocky hillsides often with Juniper and other scrub vegetation.

Edible Uses
The roots are Springparsley's main edible part. Taking on a storage/tap root orientation, they reach depths of 1'–2'. Parsnip–like, mild, and not too fibrous, they are fine eaten raw, or more so, if first cooked. They're a good carbohydrate source.

The foliage and seeds tend to be mildly bitter and/or aromatic...edible, but, best if first simmered and rinsed.

Medicinal Uses, Cautions, & Special Note
Cymopterus glomeratus (Chimaja), is the best–known spice–medicinal species. Its leaves are used as a cilantro–like garnish; its seeds, as a mild spice–carminative.

There are no cautions for Springparsley's edible use. However, Poison hemlock and Water hemlock are also in the Carrot family. Although these two plants are found in moist/disturbed soils, young growth can resemble Springparsley. Be very sure the correct plant is being harvested.

It's worth mentioning that Cymopterus is called Springparsley for good reason. April to May (sometimes June, if found at higher elevations) is the plant's above–ground window. It emerges, flowers, and sets seed all in about 3–4 weeks; after which every trace of the plant vanishes until next year.

Sustenance Index: Medium
Pictured: *Cymopterus terebinthinus* (top) | *Cymopterus longipes* (bottom)

SUMMER **FRUIT**

Thimbleberry
Rubus parviflorus

Other Common Names
Western thimbleberry

Range & Habitat
Thimbleberry's main territory constitutes the Rocky Mountains and higher mountains of the Pacific states.

In Idaho, it's reliably found throughout the sub-ranges – Bitterroot Mountains, Caribou Range, Sawtooth Range, etc. Look for the plant in dappled shade from Aspen and conifers. It's largely non-existent throughout the Plains and non-forested basins and bottomlands.

Edible Uses
Ripening mid to late summer, Thimbleberry's fruit tastes similar to Raspberry, yet not quite as succulent. They are fine eaten fresh – the drupelets peeled away from the drupe core. They too can be dried for future use or prepared as a jam/jelly.

Thimbleberry is like Raspberry in nutritional aspects. It contains good amounts of vitamin C, potassium, and magnesium.

Medicinal Uses
Thimbleberry leaf is used as a Raspberry leaf replacement. Drink the tea as urinary tract soother and female reproductive astringent.

Cautions
There are no cautions for Thimbleberry.

Special Note
Though Blackberry, Raspberry, and Thimbleberry are closely related (Rubus genus), Thimbleberry is the only plant of the bunch with a simple leaf (it is not comprised of multiple leaflets). Blackberry is 5-parted; Raspberry is 3-parted.

Sustenance Index: Medium
Pictured: *Rubus parviflorus*

SPRING–SUMMER–FALL STALK/ROOT

Thistle
Cirsium spp.

Other Common Names
Canada thistle, Bull thistle, Prairie thistle, Meadow thistle, etc.

Range & Habitat
About a dozen species of thistle are found throughout Idaho. Common to most elevations, one unifying location characteristic for all species is: disturbed soils. Look for Thistle on dirt roadsides, ditches, trailsides, stock–used meadows, and field edges.

Edible Uses
The taproot of first year or early second year plants (leaves still a basal rosette) will be found crisp and crunchy with an almost nutty flavor (species variable). As the plant ages (and develops a stalk) the root quickly becomes fibrous, woody, and inedible. Gathered during the proper time the root is fine raw, but can also be chopped, cooked, and seasoned accordingly.

Thistle stalk also deserve mention as it is an often overlooked edible. It needs to be young, just–emerging, and flexible. Cut the stalk from the base of the plant. Remove the leaves and tops (usually spiny) and peel away the outer layer until the inner palatable part is revealed. The stalk core is mild tasting and can be eaten raw, cooked, or even pickled. The larger species of Thistle (Bull thistle for instance) will be best for stalk uses.

Medicinal Uses & Cautions
There are no significant medicinal uses for Thistle. Edible thistles are unrelated in use to Milk thistle (*Silybum marianum*), a useful herbal medicine for the liver.

A number of Thistle species are listed as noxious weeds. Before collection be sure herbicides have not recently been used.

Sustenance Index: Medium
Pictured: *Cirsium scariosum*

SPRING–SUMMER | ROOT

Tuber Starwort
Pseudostellaria jamesiana

Other Common Names
Sticky starwort

Range & Habitat
Tuber starwort is an herbaceous perennial of the Middle and Southern Rockies. The plant prefers drier exposures with dappled shade, often in association with conifers and Aspen.

Edible Uses
The small tuberous rhizomes are the main food item. They lie not far below the ground's surface, which makes their procurement easy – often hands alone can be used. Once the stringy part of the rhizome is removed the tubers are fine consumed fresh (mild tasting and crunchy). They too can be wrapped in foil and baked like a potato if a warm–starchy meal is desired. Due to the plant's abundance and carbohydrate content, it's an under–appreciated wild food. The foliage too can be eaten...but it's nothing to write home about.

Medicinal Uses & Cautions
There are no significant medicinal uses or cautions for Tuber starwort.

Special Note
When not in flower, at first glance, the above–ground portion of Tuber starwort appears like so many other mountain herbs. However, some key differences that help in identification are as follows: leaves form directly opposite from each other, they are sessile (lack leaf stems) and lance–shaped. Also, each leaf pair is usually offset 30–45 degrees from the previous set. If still in doubt, just dig up a patch – small crunchy tubers connected to thin rhizomes? If so, it's Tuber starwort.

Sustenance Index: Medium
Pictured: *Pseudostellaria jamesiana*

ALL YEAR | **ENTIRE PLANT**

Tule
Schoenoplectus acutus (Scirpus acutus), S. tabernaemontani

Other Common Names
Common tule, Hardstem bulrush, Softstem bulrush

Range & Habitat
Schoenoplectus acutus and S. tabernaemontani are the two main Tule species in Idaho, though S. tabernaemontani is more commonly referred to as Softstem bulrush. No matter, they have similar morphologies and are utilized the same. Marsh, lake, and reservoir margins are common habitats for Tule.

Edible Uses
Almost all parts are utilized. The springtime emerging young stems/shoots are eaten raw or cooked. After the stems have matured, they are cut at the base and peeled of their outer sheathing layers. This exposes each stem base's tender edible core. Tule's rhizomes are edible, though the younger budding ends are the choice part. They need little preparation. The older rhizome should be peeled and cooked first due age-related toughness/sponginess. Indians would also dry these parts and grind them into a flour for later use. Both Tule pollen (knock the flowering clusters in a bucket) and seeds (post flowering) are collected and utilized in various ways. Tule pollen is high in protein and can be mixed with other flours in baking or simply combined with water and eaten as a gruel. Grind the seeds (also high in protein) and eat accordingly.

Cautions & Special Note
If consuming the rhizomes raw, consider a diluted chlorine bleach soak: mix 1 tablespoon of unscented chlorine bleach (regular Clorox) in 1 gallon of potable water. Soak the plant material in the solution for 15 minutes. Rinse and eat. Though the rhizome is smaller, other Schoenoplectus species (Bulrush) are edible as well. Mats, baskets, and even primitive garments were once woven from the mature stems of both Tule and Bulrush.

Sustenance Index: High
Pictured: *Schoenoplectus acutus var. occidentalis*

SPRING | HERBACEOUS PARTS

Tumble Mustard
Sisymbrium altissimum

Other Common Names
Tall mustard, Hedge mustard, Jim Hill mustard, Wild mustard

Range & Habitat
A common annual found throughout Idaho, Tumble mustard is also the most likely encountered western mountain state Sisymbrium species. Look for it in disturbed soils. Dirt parking lot edges, trailsides, dry cattle tanks, and drainages where some moisture has lingered are some of its usual places.

Edible Uses
The young leaves and tops (flowers and young seed pods) are best eaten as a spicy garnish or salad addition. For the consumption of larger amounts, be sure to steam/sauté these parts first. Heat dissipates much of the plant's Mustard oils, enabling greater quantities to be eaten.

Tumble mustard is a little more coarse and hairy than Watercress and Wintercress. However, once cooked, differences between the three plants are minimal.

Medicinal Uses & Cautions
Like all Mustard species, Tumble mustard contains ample amounts of glucosinolates (Mustard oil). Responsible for the plant's spicy taste, this constituent group tends to be relieving to indigestion (small handful of the fresh plant), and for women, stimulating to menses (larger amounts). Too much of the fresh plant will irritate the gastrointestinal tract and occasionally the kidneys.

Special Note
For the dedicated, the small seeds can be used as a Mustard seed replacement; however, they are very tiny and may not be worth the effort.

Sustenance Index: Low
Pictured: *Sisymbrium altissimum*

SUMMER | **FRUIT**

Utah Honeysuckle
Lonicera utahensis

Other Common Names
Red twinberry, Fly honeysuckle

Range & Habitat
Utah honeysuckle is principally a plant of the Middle and Northern Rockies. In Idaho, it's mostly found at subalpine elevations with Fir, Spruce, and Aspen. It's an occasional sub-shrub preferring dappled shade areas next to streams and drainages.

Edible Uses
The red berries are juicy and semi-sweet – not at all bad tasting. Eat them fresh (insignificant seeds) as a trail snack or dry them for later as an addition to other dried fruit and nuts. If enough of the fruit is available, they also make a fine jelly/preserve base.

Medicinal Uses
The flowers and leaves are similar in use to Japanese honeysuckle (Lonicera japonica): use the infusion as a mild antiviral diaphoretic during cold and flu season. Most Lonicera species can be used this way and are related to Elder (same family) in application.

Cautions & Special Note
There are no cautions for the fruit (Lonicera utahensis). A couple of other native species of Honeysuckle are found in Idaho. L. involucrata (Twinberry) is a bush. It has a non-edible bitter-tasting black berry (not poisonous per se, but very poor tasting). L. ciliosa (Orange honeysuckle) has a clustered red berry. I'm assuming it's bitter like most other Honeysuckles of similar form. L. caerulea var. cauriana (Fly honeysuckle) grows occasionally in the Salmon River Mountains. It's closely related to Haskap (a collection of Eurasian varieties of L. caerulea). Overseas Haskap berries are a well-known edible. The million-dollar-question – is var. cauriana (red berry) as edible as Haskap (blue berry). It's doubtful. Tasting is believing. Try a couple if encountered. Even if poor-tasting, chewing a berry or two won't hurt.

Sustenance Index: Medium
Pictured: *Lonicera utahensis*

SPRING–SUMMER   **HERBACEOUS PARTS**

Watercress
Nasturtium officinale (Rorippa nasturtium–aquaticum)

Other Common Names
Creek mustard, Berro

Range & Habitat
Common throughout most of North America, look for this naturalized semi–aquatic perennial along gently flowing streams and springs.

Edible Uses
Like other mustards, Watercress makes a nice addition to foraged salads and mixed greens. It is warming and spicy, and as an accent, is pleasantly stimulating to the palate. Most people find a mouth full of fresh Watercress too spicy; however, larger quantities can be eaten if first boiled or steamed.

Medicinal Uses
A small handful is useful for stomach bloating and indigestion.

Cautions
Large amounts of fresh Watercress can irritate the kidneys, and in some women, stimulate menses.

Special Note
Watercress is one of the better tasting mustards. It has a well-deserved reputation as a leafy edible. Unlike true Mustard (Brassica or Sinapis), which is best known as the seed (and Mustard greens) source for the condiment, Watercress has a longer picking/eating season due to the extra hydration provided by water environs.

Before collecting any water–thriving plant, be aware of the water's quality. Agricultural/industrial runoff, cattle activity, and so on, can adversely affect the water and local plant life. If microorganisms are suspected, a diluted chlorine bleach soak then rinse is wise. *See Tule.*

Sustenance Index: Low
Pictured: *Nasturtium officinale*

52

SPRING | **ENTIRE PLANT**

Western Spring Beauty
Claytonia lanceolata

Other Common Names
Lanceleaf spring beauty

Range & Habitat
Western spring beauty is a little perennial of Idaho's middle elevations. The plant is most commonly found in grassy patches and loamy soils in association with Aspen and Maple. It's not a plant of shady coniferous forests, but of open/dappled exposures.

Edible Uses
All parts of Western spring beauty are edible. Its semi–succulent foliage is fine consumed raw or once steamed or sautéed and seasoned accordingly.

The plant's root (small tuberous corms), is its main edible portion. Containing ample carbohydrates, it will be found more sustaining than the above ground parts. They do not lie far below the ground's surface, which makes collecting easy. Once unearthed and peeled, the roots are fine eaten raw, as they are bland and mild in taste, or better yet, cooked and seasoned first. One simple method is to add a bouillon cube to a handful of corms and wrap everything together in foil. Place the foil packet over campfire coals for 5–10 minutes or until cooked; remove and eat. Delicious!

Medicinal Uses, Cautions, & Special Note
There are no medicinal uses for Western spring beauty. Eating large amounts of the raw foliage (oxalates) may irritate the kidneys. Boiling and rinsing the leaves first will negate this potential.

The plant is nearly impossible to locate once its flowering season has past (early–mid spring). Bitterroot, Miner's lettuce, and Western spring beauty are all related. Edible qualities for these plants are similar.

Sustenance Index: Medium
Pictured: *Claytonia lanceolata*

SPRING–SUMMER | **ENTIRE PLANT**

Wild Onion
Allium spp.

Other Common Names
Tapertip onion, Twincrest onion, Brandegee's onion, Nodding onion, Geyer's onion, and so forth

Range & Habitat
Idaho is home to over a dozen onion species. Allium acuminatum (Tapertip onion), A. cernuum (Nodding onion), and A. geyeri (Geyer's onion) are a few of the more abundant species. They populate a variety of habitats – forests, hillsides, and meadows.

Edible Uses
All Wild onion species are distinguishable from other monocots by their distinctive onion scent. The entire plant – leaf, flower stalk (scape), flowers, and bulb are equally edible. The bulb usually has the strongest flavor; the herbaceous portions – the mildest.

All parts can be eaten fresh (limited); however, for the consumption of larger amounts, Wild onion should first be cooked/baked. This will remove much of its harshness. Wrapped in foil with a bouillon cube and then set on campfire coals for 5–10 minutes is a fine way to proceed.

Medicinal Uses, Cautions, & Special Note
In terms of medicinal strength, Wild onion can be thought of as a diminutive Garlic (another Allium). A Wild onion honey steep makes a serviceable cold and flu application. It will be found mildly antibacterial and antiviral. Too much raw Wild onion will cause digestive upset.

If it looks like Wild onion, yet has no onion smell, unless properly identified as another edible plant, then do not eat it. The plant is not Wild onion, but likely a related plant – some of which are edible, but some too are toxic (for instance, Deathcamas).

Sustenance Index: Medium
Pictured: *Allium cernuum* (top) | *Allium acuminatum* (bottom)

SUMMER–FALL | **FRUIT**

Wild Rose
Rosa acicularis, R. gymnocarpa, R. nutkana, R. woodsii

Other Common Names
Prickly rose, Dwarf rose, Nootka rose, Woods' rose

Range & Habitat
Four wild species of Rosa are found throughout Idaho. They are mostly associated with mountain–conifer–Aspen elevations. Wood's rose (Rosa woodsii) is the most abundant and is reliably encountered state–wide.

Edible Uses
The fruit of Wild rose (any Rose species) is called a 'hip'. Ripening late summer to early fall, they can be eaten fresh, but are not the best tasting: seed–filled/insipid. Their best preparation is as a jelly or syrup base.

Wild rose hips' high vitamin content makes it an important forage if nutritional deficiency (especially vitamin C) is suspected. For this reason, the dried hips were an important cold–season food supplement, especially if the diet was limited (cabin shut–in: canned food/jerky/beans/etc.). Relatedly, crushed hips were a common pemmican ingredient.

Medicinal Uses
The encapsulated hip powder (or simply mixed with water), taken internally, is nutritional (especially vitamin C, minerals, and health–promoting lipids). The hip powder is also broadly antiinflammatory and tissue/skin supportive. The leaves are mildly astringent and used as a poultice on minor bites, stings, and burns.

Cautions & Special Note
Wild rose is caution–free. Cultivated Rose hips (similar vitamin C and nutritional qualities) are used the same as wild species.

Sustenance Index: Medium
Pictured: *Rosa woodsii*

SUMMER · FRUIT

Wild Strawberry
Fragaria vesca, F. virginiana

Other Common Names
Woodland strawberry, Virginia strawberry

Range & Habitat
Range and habitat (and physical characteristics) for both species are essentially interchangeable, with Virginia strawberry being the more populous of the two.

Common throughout all of Idaho's higher elevations, Wild strawberry is most often found in dappled shade with Fir, Spruce, and/or Aspen overhead.

Edible Uses
The edibility of Wild strawberry needs little explanation; they are just as tasty as garden-grown or store-bought Strawberry (usually the cultivar – Fragaria X ananassa).

Eat the fruit fresh, dehydrated for later, or prepared as a jam/jelly or preserve. Like the cultivated type, Wild strawberry is high in potassium and contains fair amounts of vitamin C. The drawbacks to Wild strawberry are its small fruit size and erratic fruit development. Plants lower in elevation are often sterile.

Medicinal Uses
Wild strawberry leaf is mildly astringent. As a topically applied poultice, it is arresting and inflammation-reducing to minor cuts and scrapes. Internally, the leaf tea is used as a substitute for Raspberry leaf tea (female reproductive tonic).

Cautions & Special Note
There are no cautions for Wild strawberry. It belongs to the Rose family and is related to Blackberry, Raspberry, Wild rose, and Thimbleberry.

Sustenance Index: Medium
Pictured: *Fragaria virginiana*

SPRING–SUMMER | **SEED**

Wild Sunflower
Helianthus annuus

Other Common Names
Western sunflower, Common sunflower, etc.

Range & Habitat
Wild Sunflower is common throughout most of Idaho (and much of America). Good places to look for the plant: roadsides, trailsides, forest openings, meadows, pastures, and floodplains.

Edible Uses
Clip the seed heads from the upper stems when they are almost fully mature and dry. After drying in a paper bag or box, garble the seeds from the seed head. Eat as is (thin hull and all) or grind/sift and utilize the seeds as a meal. High in protein and essential oils, they are very nutritious.

The very young flower buds are snipped from the stems and simmered for 10–15 minutes. Rinsed and seasoned, they make a fair cooked vegetable.

Medicinal Uses
There are no medicinal uses for Wild sunflower.

Cautions
There are no cautions for Wild sunflower.

Special Note
Wild species are also a favorite of birds – if you wait until the seed heads are completely dry on the plant before collecting, they will be eaten.

Garden varieties of Sunflower are cultivars. They have been selected and bred over the years to produce the sunflower seed of commerce.

Jerusalem artichoke is also a Sunflower (*Helianthus tuberosus*) of sorts. But unlike Wild sunflower, Jerusalem artichoke is cultivated for its edible tuberous root.

Sustenance Index: High
Pictured: *Helianthus annuus*

SPRING–SUMMER — **HERBACEOUS PARTS**

Wintercress
Barbarea vulgaris, B. orthoceras

Other Common Names
Yellow rocket, American wintercress, Erectpod wintercress

Range & Habitat
Two Wintercress species are found in Utah – non-native Barbarea vulgaris, and native B. orthoceras. The native species is a bit more common than the other. Both are almost always found in the moist soils of meadows and streamsides.

Edible Uses
Like others in the Mustard family, Wintercress has a pronounced spicy-pungent-mustard taste. The young leaves, flowers, and immature seed pods are consumed fresh, in small amounts, as a salad accent or garnish. Boiled or sautéed briefly, greater quantities can be eaten without the occasional irritating qualities of the fresh plant – heat dissipates most of the plant's mustard oils.

Medicinal Uses
Eat a small handful of the fresh leaf if suffering from indigestion (not heartburn). Many find its stimulating nature relieving to gastric stasis and bloating.

Cautions & Special Note
For women, too much of the fresh plant may stimulant menses. Additionally, I've observed large amounts of the fresh plant cause kidney sensitivity and stomach unease. The causative principles for this are known as glucosinolates, a group of volatiles common to most Mustard family plants. Small amounts of these compounds are fine; large amounts are irritating. Another mountain/moist-soil growing Mustard found in Idaho is Yellowcress (Rorippa spp.). It too is herbaceous with yellow flowers and elongated seedpods. In terms of edibility, it can be treated the same as Wintercress.

Sustenance Index: Low
Pictured: *Barbarea vulgaris*

SPRING | **ENTIRE PLANT**

Yellow Fritillary
Fritillaria pudica

Other Common Names
Yellow bells, Yellow missionbells

Range & Habitat
Fairly common in Idaho and surrounding northwestern/western states, Yellow fritillary is a basin–scrub–meadow–grassland plant. Occasionally it's found in and around open woods, but still a full sun exposures is an important aspect in its habitat.

Edible Uses
From flower and stem to root bulb, all parts of Yellow fritillary are edible. The buds, flowers, young seed pods, stems, and leaves are eaten without killing the plant. As a cooked green or fresh, they tender (generally) and pleasant tasting.

The bulbs require slightly more effort to procure. They are often ½′ or so beneath the ground's surface, so digging with a trowel is necessary. The bulbs provide more sustenance than the upper parts due to their greater carbohydrate content. They are pleasant tasting (but starchy). Eat them raw or cooked.

An important wild food supplemental item, most tribes (Blackfoot, Flathead, Goshute, Salish, and others) utilized the plant at one time or another.

Medicinal Uses, Cautions, & Special Note
Yellow fritillary has no medicinal use nor are there cautions associated with the plant.

Idaho is home to another fritillary species, that of Fritillaria atropurpurea (Spotted fritillary). Occasionally this species is listed as (mildly) toxic; however, I tend to doubt this because of its relationship to the profiled species. Anyway, approach munching away on Spotted fritillary with a bit of caution.

Sustenance Index: High
Pictured: *Fritillaria pudica*

SPRING | **LEAF/STEM**

Yellowdock
Rumex crispus

Other Common Names
Curly dock, Narrowleaf dock

Range & Habitat
Yellowdock is common state-wide. It's almost always encountered in moist-disturbed soils. Lake, pond, and stream sides, cattle tanks, and other areas where the ground remains hydrated are good place to look for Yellowdock.

Edible Uses
Yellowdock makes for a fair green. The younger leaves and flexible stems are palatable raw (similar to the texture of kale or chard); however, they're better if first sautéed or steamed. Some plants will be more sour/tart than others – this is mainly due to calcium oxalate content within the leaf/stem.

Medicinal Uses
Yellowdock is considered the most important medicinal species of the genus. It's a root medicine and has therapeutic effects that influence the liver, intestines, and skin.

Cautions
There are only minor cautions for the consumption of Yellowdock greens. For some people the oxalate content may be irritating to the kidneys, but this is only a problem if consumed raw in large quantities.

Special Note
Native to Eurasia, Yellowdock is now grows worldwide. In many areas it is considered invasive. It is likely one of the oldest non-native plants found in North America. 'Crispus' refers to the leaves' crinkled edges.

Sustenance Index: Low
Pictured: *Rumex crispus*

SUMMER | **TUBER**

Yampah
Perideridia bolanderi, P. gairdneri

Other Common Names
Bolander's yampah, Gardener's yampah

Range & Habitat
Two species of Yampah are found in Idaho. Bolander's yampah mainly inhabits the central-western part of the state (dry soils). Gardener's yampah is more widespread. It tends to grow along streamsides and/or in stream-hydrated meadows.

Edible Uses
The seed, flower, leaf, and stem are eaten raw; however, the small tubers are the sought-after part. They lie just below the ground's surface and are small: 1"–2" long, slender (usually), with 1-6 tubers (species dependent) per plant. Eaten freely, they are pleasantly crunchy (not fibrous). I can't seem to keep form eating them immediately, but I'm sure they too are a fine cooking candidate.

Medicinal Uses & Cautions
There are no medicinal uses or cautions for Yampah's internal consumption.

Special Note
If the tubers do not look like what is pictured...do not eat them! It's possible you have collected the wrong (and poisonous) plant. Yampah is small (1'–3' high), very slender, delicate, with parted spear-linear leaves (vein travels to the leaflet tip). Water Hemlock (deadly) is a larger plant, usually growing directly in water with larger/toothed leaves (leaflet vein travels to the cut). Its roots are larger and clustered. They occasionally have inner hollow compartments. Poison hemlock (deadly) is too a large plant, but has fern-like leaves, with a semi-woody taproot. To eliminate mistakes, wait until Yampah is fully developed and in flower (summer) before it is gathered.

Sustenance Index: High
Pictured: *Perideridia parishii*

Index

A

Acer glabrum 27
    grandidentatum 27
    negundo 27
Achnatherum hymenoides 24
Alder-leaf serviceberry 42
Allium acuminatum 54
    cernuum 54
    geyeri 54
Alpine bitterroot 8
Amaranth 4, 25, 34
Amaranthus 4
Amelanchier alnifolia 42
    utahensis 42
American red raspberry 39
    wintercress 58
anthocyanins 5
antioxidant 5, 23
antiviral 16, 51
Artocarpus altilis 31
    heterophyllus 31
Ash leaf maple 27
Asparagus 5, 10
    officinalis 5
Atriplex hortensis 34
    micrantha 34
    rosea 34
Autumn olive 40
Avalanche lily 19

B

Balsam poplar 29
Barbarea orthoceras 58
    vulgaris 58
Barestem biscuitroot 7
Beeplant 6
Bee spiderflower 6
berberine 22
Berberis aquifolium 22
    nervosa 22
    repens 22
Berro 52
Bilberry 23
Birdweed 13
Biscuitroot 7
Bitterroot 8, 29, 53
Blackberry 9, 39, 46, 56
Black currant 15
    gooseberry 20
    hawthorn 21
Blueberry 23
Blue elderberry 16
Bolander's yampah 59, 61
Box elder 27
Bracken fern 10
Breadfruit 31
Bull thistle 47

C

California nettle 33
Callirhoe involucrata 12
Calochortus elegans 28
    eurycarpus 28
    gunnisonii 28
    macrocarpus 28
    nitidus 28
    nuttallii 28
Camas 11, 19
Camash 11
Canada thistle 47
Canadian gooseberry 20
capers 6
Carrotleaf desertparsley 7
Cascade oregongrape 22
Checkermallow 12, 26
Cheeseplant 26
Cheeseweed 26
Chenopodium album 25
    ambrosioides 25
    berlandieri 25
    fremontii 25
Cherry 14
Chickenweed 13
Chick plant 13
Chickweed 13, 37
Chimaja 45
Chokecherry 14
Chrysanthemum cinerariaefolium 35
Cirsium spp. 47
Clammyweed 6
Claytonia lanceolata 53
    perfoliata 29
Cleome serrulata 6
Colorado 21
Common asparagus 5
Common mallow 26
    monkey flower 30
    sow thistle 44
    sunflower 57
Cous biscuitroot 7
Crataegus douglasii 21
    rivularis 21
Creek mustard 52
Creeping hollygrape 22
Curly dock 60
Currant 15, 20
Cut-leaf blackberry 9
cyanogenic glycosides 16
Cymopterus spp. 45

D

Dalmatian daisy 35
Deathcamas 11, 54, 55
Desert gooseberry 20
Desertparsley 7
Dewberry 39
diaphoretic 51
Disporum trachycarpum 17
Dogtooth fawn lily 19
Dwarf bilberry 23
Dwarf rose 55
Dysphania ambrosioides 25

E

Eastern chokecherry 14
Elaeagnus angustifolia 40
    umbellata 40
Elder 16, 51
Elderberry syrup 16
Epazote 25
Erectpod wintercress 58
Erythronium grandiflorum 19

F

Fairybells 17
False Solomon's Seal 17
Fanweed 18
Fendler's springparsley 45
Fennel 7
fever 16
Fiddleneck 10
Field daisy 35
    sorrel 43
Field pennycress 18
Fir 39
flu 16, 51
Fly honeysuckle 51
Fragaria vesca 56
    virginiana 56
    X ananassa 56
Frenchweed 18
Fringed mariposa lily 28

G

Garden asparagus 5
Gardener's yampah 61
Garden orach 34
Garlic 54
gastrointestinal 38
Geyer's onion 54
Glacier lily 19
glucosinolates 6, 58
Goat's beard 41
Golden currant 15
Gooseberry 15, 20

Goosefoot 25
Gordolobo 32
Great ox-eye 35
   Plains 12
Grouse whortleberry 23

H

Hardstem bulrush 49
Hawthorn 21
Hedge mustard 50
Helianthus annuus 57
   tuberosus 57
High blood pressure 21
Himalayan blackberry 9
Hollygrape 22

I

Indian lettuce 29
   millet 24
   mountain ricegrass 24

J

Jackfruit 31
Japanese 51
   honeysuckle 51
Jerusalem artichoke 57
Juniper 29, 42, 45

L

Lambsquarters 25, 34
Lanceleaf spring beauty 53
Lanté 38
Leucanthemum vulgare 35
Lewisia nevadensis 8
   pygmaea 8
   rediviva 8
   triphylla 8
Lily family 19
Lomatium bicolor 7
   cous 7
   dissectum 7
   foeniculaceum 7
   nevadense 7
   nudicaule 7
   triternatum 7
Lonicera caerulea 51
   japonica 51
   utahensis 51

M

magnesium 9, 23, 46
Maianthemum racemosum 17
   stellatum 17
Mallow 12, 26

Malva neglecta 26
Mariposa lily 19, 28
Meadow salsify 41
Meadow thistle 47
Mimulus glabratus 30
   guttatus 30
Miner's lettuce 8, 29
   family 8
Monkey flower 30, 44
Montiaceae 8
Moraceae 31
Morus spp. 31
Mouse ear 13
Mulberry 31
Mullein 32
Mustard 6, 50, 58
   family 58
   greens 52
   oils 58
   seed 52

N

Narrowleaf dock 60
Nasturtium officinale 52
Nettle 33, 37
Nevada bitterroot 8
Nineleaf springparsley 7
Nodding onion 54
Nootka rose 55
Northern currant 15

O

Okra 12, 26
Oleaster 40
Orach 34
Oregon 8
   bitterroot 8
   checkerbloom 12
Oregongrape 22
Oryzopsis hymenoides 24
oxalates 4, 8, 25, 29, 34, 43, 53, 60
Ox-eye daisy 35
Oyster root 41

P

Pacific blackberry 9
   Northwest 23
Panicgrass 36
Panicum capillare 36
Parietaria spp. 37
Pellitory 37
   of-the-wall 37
pemmican 55
Pennsylvania pellitory 37
Peppergrass 18
Perideridia spp. 59, 60, 61

Peritoma serrulata 6
Pigweed 4
Plantago major 38
   ovata 38
Plantain 38
Poison hemlock 61, 61
Ponderosa pine 12, 32
   potassium 23, 46
Powell's amaranth 4
Prairie thistle 47
Prickly rose 55
Prosartes trachycarpa 17
Prunus serotina 14
   virginiana var. demissa 14
   var. melanocarpa 14
Pseudostellaria jamesiana 48
Pteridium aquilinum 10
Purple salsify 41
Purslane 29
Pygmy bitterroot 8

Q

Quamash 11
Quelites 25

R

Raspberry 9, 21, 39, 46, 56
Red mulberry 31
   sorrel 43
Ribes aureum 15
   cereum 15
   hudsonianum 15
   inerme 20
   lacustre 20
   laxiflorum 15
   montigenum 20
   nigrum 15
   oxyacanthoides 20
   velutinum 20
   viscosissimum 15
Rillita pellitory 37
River hawthorn 21
Rocky Mountain beeplant 6
Rocky Mountains 6, 39, 42, 46, 51
Rorippa nasturtium-aquaticum 52
Rosa nutkana 55
   woodsii 55
Rose 14, 21, 42, 55, 56
Rough-fruited fairy-bells 17
   mandarin 17
Roundleaf monkey flower 30
Rubus armeniacus 9
   idaeus 39
   laciniatus 9
   parviflorus 46
   ursinus 9

Rumex acetosella 43
   crispus 60
   hymenosepalus 60
Russian mulberry 31
   olive 40
   orach 34

S

Salmonberry 39
Salsify 41
Saltbush 34
samaras 27
sambucine 16
Sambucus cerulea 16
   glauca 16
   neomexicana 16
   nigra ssp. cerulea 16
San Juans 46
Schoenoplectus acutus 49
   tabernaemontani 49
Seep monkey flower 30
Serviceberry 21, 42
Sheep's sorrel 43
Sidalcea candida 12
   oregana 12
Sierra bitterroot 8
Silkworm mulberry 31
Silky mountain rice 24
Silver Berry 40
Silybum marianum 47
Sisymbrium altissimum 50
Small camas 11
Softstem bulrush 49
Sonchus 44
   asper 44
   oleraceus 44
Sorrel 43
Sow thistle 44
Spiny sow thistle 44
Spring beauty 8, 29, 53
Springparsley 7, 45
Spruce 39
Star Solomon's Seal 17
Stellaria media 13
Sticky currant 15
   starwort 48
Stinging nettle 33
Stinkweed 18
Stipa hymenoides 24
Strawberry 56

T

Tall mustard 50
tannins 40
Tapertip onion 54
Thimbleberry 9, 39, 46, 56
Thistle 47

Thlaspi arvense 18
Three-leaved lewisia 8
Ticklegrass 36
Toxicoscordion 11
Tragopogon dubius 41
   porrifolius 41
   pratensis 41
Tuber starwort 48
Tule 49, 52
Tumble mustard 50
   panic 36
Tumbleweed amaranth 4
Tumbling orach 34
Twinberry 51
Twincrest onion 54

U

urinary tract 43
Urtica dioica ssp. gracilis 33
Utah 42
   honeysuckle 51

V

Vaccinium caespitosum 23
   corymbosum 23
   myrtillus 23
   scoparium 23
Verbascum thapsus 32
Virginia strawberry 56
vitamin A 23, 25
   B 21, 23, 39
   C 15, 20, 21, 23, 39, 46, 55, 56
   E 39

W

Watercress 30, 52
Water hemlock 61, 61
Wax currant 15
Western bracken fern 10
   chokecherry 14
   elder 16
   red raspberry 39
   spring beauty 8, 29, 53
   sunflower 57
   thimbleberry 46
White checkersbloom 12
   mulberry 31
Whitestem gooseberry 20
Whortleberry 23
Wild cherry 14
   lettuce 44
   mustard 50
   olive 40
   onion 54
   rose 55
   strawberry 56

   sunflower 57
Winecup 12
Wintercress 6, 50
Witchgrass 36
Woodland strawberry 56
Woolly mullein 32

Y

Yampah 59, 61
Yellowdock 60
Yellow fritillary 19, 59
   monkey flower 30
   rocket 58
   salsify 41